bouncing back

WHAT DO YOU KNOW ABOUT COPING WITH STRESS?
TAKE THIS QUIZ NOW—AND THEN AFTER YOU'VE READ
THE BOOK, TAKE IT AGAIN, COMPARE YOUR ANSWERS,
AND FIND OUT WHAT YOU'VE LEARNED!

True or False?

1 Stress only affects certain people.

2 The key to coping with stress is to ignore it as much as possible.

3 Resiliency is the ability to cope with and adapt to the stresses in life.

4 Some people are just naturally better at coping with stress than others.

5 Reading is not an effective way of coping with stress.

6 Volunteering is one way to reduce stress.

7 Resilient people know how to safely escape from their troubles on a temporary basis.

8 If you're a person who naturally freaks out from stress, there's very little you can do about it.

Answer key: (1) False; (2) False; (3) True; (4) False; (5) False; (6) True; (7) True; (8) False

Learning to take it one step at a time ...

Photographs © 2007: Alamy Images: 5 top, 61 (Jeff Greenberg), 9 (Terry Oakley), 5 bottom, 66 (PhotoAlto), 49 (Janine Weidel/Photolibrary); Corbis Images: 2 (Darama), 91 (Mitchell Gerber), 93 (Roy Morsch/zefa), 99 (Nancy Ney), 26 (H. Armstrong Roberts), 88, 97 (Royalty-Free), 60 (Flip Schulke), 68 (Tom Stewart/zefa), 21 (Turbo/zefa); Getty Images: 100 (Dennis Galante/ Stone), 19 (Alex Mares-Manton/Asia Images), 41 (Stephen Munday), 39 (Gen Nishino/Taxi), cover background (Photodisc Green), 89 (photos Alyson/Taxi), 28 (Darren Robb/The Image Bank), 52 (Donn Thompson/DK Stock), 63 (Dougal Waters/Photographer's Choice), 4, 15 (Brad Wilson/Photonica), 54 background (Yellow Dog Productions/The Image Bank); JupiterImages/Jean-Louis Bellurget: 44; Kobal Collection/Picture Desk/New World Pix: 27; Masterfile: 24 (Kathleen Finlay), 6 (Rick Gomez), 35 (WireImageStock); Monty Stilson: cover; Muscular Dystrophy Association of the United States: 72; photolibrary.com/Elea Dumas/ Nonstock: 65; VEER: 29 (Digital Vision Photography), 76, 94 (Image Source Photography), 84 (Stockbyte).

Cover design: Marie O'Neill
Book production: The Design Lab.

Library of Congress Cataloging-in-Publication Data
Jones, Jami L.
  Bouncing back : dealing with the stuff life throws at you / Jami L.
Jones.
    p. cm. — (Choices)
  Includes bibliographical references and index.
  ISBN-13: 978-0-531-12404-8 (lib. bdg.)   978-0-531-17730-3 (pbk.)
  ISBN-10: 0-531-12404-5 (lib. bdg.)   0-531-17730-0 (pbk.)
  1. Resilience (Personality trait) I. Title. II. Series: Choices
(Franklin Watts, Inc.)
  BF698.35.R47J66 2005
  155.2'4—dc22   2004018426

1 2 3 4 5 6 7 8 9 10 R 16 15 14 13 12 11 10 09 08 07

SCHOLASTIC
CHOICES™

Dealing
with the
stuff life
throws
at you

bouncing
back

Jami L. Jones

Franklin Watts®

A DIVISION OF SCHOLASTIC INC.
NEW YORK • TORONTO • LONDON • AUCKLAND • SYDNEY
MEXICO CITY • NEW DELHI • HONG KONG
DANBURY, CONNECTICUT

i'm stressed out!

Meredith, 14

i'm stressed out!

"I'M SINKING FAST . . . I NEED HELP."

Meredith's Story

Meredith has been really stressed out. "I'm in a wedding in less than thirty-six hours, and the rest of my life has been pretty messed up. I get really sick of people telling me that everything is going to be OK, and then other people saying it's all going to get harder. I already know that it gets harder, not easier. I'm sinking fast . . . I need help."

The stress that Meredith feels is familiar to most teens. She's feeling stressed out because she doesn't have a plan to deal with her challenges and problems—they're taking control. Stress can be an overwhelming feeling.

Are you stressed out? Do you feel overwhelmed by challenges and problems? If so, you aren't alone. Stress is part of everybody's life. The problems that tend to stress out teens like you include:

- **school**
- negative self-image
- **changes in your body**
- unsafe neighborhoods
- **separation/divorce of parents**
- illness or death in the family
- **family problems, including financial**
- moving/changing schools
- **too many activities**
- having too high expectations

Source: www.focusas.com/Stress.html

Stress is part of life and can never be completely eliminated. The key to coping with it is resiliency.

resiliency

the ability to recover quickly from illness, change, or misfortune

Being resilient means taking stress in stride because you already have a game plan to handle what is going on in your life. Here's an analogy that shows you how resiliency can work:

Visualize a bouncing ball. The pressure of the air inside the ball causes it to bounce. When a ball is thrown against the floor, the air inside acts as a spring to push it back into a round shape.

Now imagine you are the bouncing ball. When you are able to bounce back from stress, it is because of resiliency. Instead of air, however, you can be full of good habits and skills that help you cope with stress. The skills for withstanding the **adversity**, or problems and challenges, in your life don't always come naturally. Luckily, you can learn many ways to bounce back!

Surprising Strength

A great deal of research has been done on the ways people cope with stress. At one time, the theory was that teens and children who were abused, neglected, or had other serious problems and challenges growing up would become dysfunctional. However, in the 1940s, new studies showed that some kids with dysfunctional families were actually healthy and well adjusted.

dysfunctional

having trouble in society, school, and home life

Then, in the 1960s, Dr. Emmy Werner, a college professor, and Ruth Smith, a clinical psychologist, began a forty-year study to get to the bottom of the question of resiliency. They studied almost five hundred people from birth to age 40. The purpose of their study was to answer two important questions:

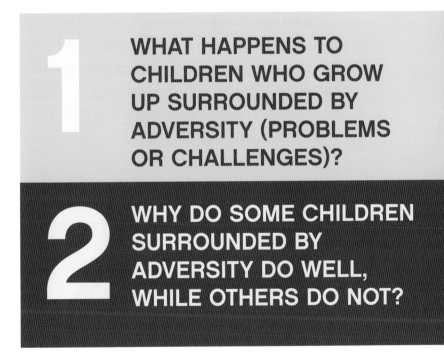

1 WHAT HAPPENS TO CHILDREN WHO GROW UP SURROUNDED BY ADVERSITY (PROBLEMS OR CHALLENGES)?

2 WHY DO SOME CHILDREN SURROUNDED BY ADVERSITY DO WELL, WHILE OTHERS DO NOT?

The Keys to Bouncing Back

One-third of the people in Werner and Smith's study were considered **high risk** because they either lived in poverty or had parents who were abusive, poorly educated, or mentally ill. They came from homes with alcoholism, fighting, or divorce. Some had health, learning, or behavior problems, causing them to do poorly in school.

To their surprise, Werner and Smith found that one-third of the high-risk kids were doing well by age 18. That did not fit with the old theories at all. Over time, the high-risk kids did even better. By age 40, more than 60 percent were doing just fine! The study labeled these people "resilient."

Studies prove that **ONE-THIRD** of kids from dysfunctional families do well by the age 18

Intrigued by their unexpected findings, the doctors focused on these resilient people. They soon found out that they had certain qualities and characteristics, called **protective factors**, that let them bounce back from stress.

MOST IMPORTANT
Protective Factors
that help you bounce back

- **Strong problem-solving skills**
- **Ability to seek help**
- **Skills in setting goals**
- **Ability to find positive role models**
- **Volunteering and helping others**
- **Ability to make and keep a few good friends**
- **Participating in hobbies and interests**
- **Competence in reading**
- **Faith in an idea or a belief, such as a religion or a philosophy**
- **Practicing good habits for staying healthy**

Between 1989 and 1996, another important study on resiliency was conducted. In Minneapolis, Minnesota, researchers surveyed more than 350,000 students in grades six through twelve in hundreds of U.S. communities. The researchers wanted to know more about the characteristics and behaviors of the healthiest children and teens as well as the most **at-risk**.

GETTING TO THE
bottom
of the BOUNCE

Researchers asked these questions about how kids deal with the many challenges they face growing up:

- Why do some teens have an **easy time** growing up, while others do not?
- Why do some teens get involved in **risky activities**, while others do not?
- Why do some teens become **resilient**, while others do not?

The researchers identified qualities that helped teens do well and named these skills **developmental assets.** Positive experiences and relationships throughout childhood help children learn healthy ways of interacting with the world around them. Developmental assets are these helpful behaviors, such as the ability to form friendships and practice self-control. The more developmental assets a person develops, the less likely he or she is to participate in risky behavior and the more likely he or she will do well in life.

who
Has Developmental Assets?
Out of all the kids researchers surveyed:

64%
felt loved and supported by their family

43%
were good at making and keeping friends

45%
felt they had control over many things

- **64% felt loved and supported by their family. Teens who are close to family members are more likely to be emotionally healthy.**
- **43% were good at making and keeping friends. One of the best ways to make friends is by joining clubs.**
- **45% felt they had control over many things that happen to them. This power comes from knowing when to say yes, how to say no, and taking responsibility for decisions.**

WHY ARE DEVELOPMENTAL ASSETS SO IMPORTANT?

provide the foundation to build your life on

act as a positive influence on the choices you make and the actions you take

increase in value over time

help you become more competent, caring, and responsible

provide a sense of security

can seriously affect you now and in the future

keep you from getting involved in risky behaviors

provide resources you can draw on again and again

make you a better person

Source: *What Teens Need to Succeed: Proven, Practical Ways to Shape Your Own Future,* by Peter L. Benson, Judy Galbraith, and Pamela Espeland

There are parts of your life you cannot control. Nobody's life is perfect. It is important to remember that there is help out there for everyone who wants to learn ways of dealing with the many stresses in their lives. Don't get discouraged if you don't have every single protective factor or developmental asset listed in this book. Learning of just a few new personal resources can help you more than you might think. While you can't control what life throws at you, you can control how you bounce back!

There are two things you should keep in mind as you read through this book:

1. Research has proven that resilient teens have one, two, three, or more of these protective factors and developmental assets.
2. The protective factors listed here are within YOUR grasp and YOUR control.

Protective Factors +
Developmental Assets

A loving, nurturing family is the number-one key to a teen's resiliency.

= Resiliency

Back to Meredith's Story

Remember Meredith from the beginning of this chapter? She was totally overwhelmed by the increasing responsibilities in her life. It can be hard to focus when everything seems to be coming at you from all directions and you feel you don't have any support. In a tough situation, it is important to realize you have more support than you think. You can draw upon the protective factors and developmental assets—your inner strength—to find new ways of coping with new stresses.

First, Meredith needs to focus on one problem at a time. The most immediate stress in her life is a confusing new experience—being in a wedding. Second, she needs to remember that it's okay to ask for help! She needs to find out what is expected of her so she can use this information to set goals that she can achieve without losing her cool. Once the wedding is over, Meredith will find that she has learned new skills that she can apply to the other stresses in her life. By breaking down her overwhelming stress into single, smaller stresses, she can tackle them one at a time.

The ability to set achievable goals is essential to being a resilient person in the face of life's many challenges. In this book, you'll find several simple, easy-to-remember tools for breaking down your own problems and setting goals to overcome them.

Remember, this is just a beginning. Go beyond this book and check out resources available at your library and school, on the Internet, and within your family and community.

After all, it is **YOUR JOB** to make life successful. In order to do that, you have to start being that bouncing ball!

Are You a resilient Person?

Keep track of your answers on a separate piece of paper and tally your score to find out.

1. How do you react to some of the most common stresses in your life?
   a. I think about them and try to figure out what I should do.
   b. I examine my schedule and see what I can do to relieve stress.
   c. I bury my head under the blankets and hope they will go away.
   d. I get mad at the people around me and tend to be hostile.

2. I go to caring, nurturing people when I feel too bogged down with life.
   a. always
   b. sometimes
   c. rarely
   d. never

3. I set expectations for myself that are:
   a. reasonable.
   b. challenging.
   c. demanding.
   d. impossible.

4. My opinions are listened to:
   a. most of the time.
   b. some of the time.
   c. only rarely.
   d. virtually never.

Answer key:

Give yourself 1 point for a answers, 2 for b, 3 for c, and 4 for d.
The higher your score, the less resilient you are.

13–16 You need to memorize this book!

7–12 You're on the right track—keep reading.

4–6 You're pretty easygoing, aren't you?

chapter two

Jasmine, 13

skills for survival

Skills for Survival

"HELP!"

Jasmine's Story

Thirteen-year-old Jasmine's life is a difficult one. "My mother is an alcoholic. I've seen what happens to alcoholics. I know the bad decisions they make. This is not what I want for my life."

Psychologist Dr. Cindy Scott offers some advice for kids like Jasmine who are afraid of making poor decisions. She says, "Just remember, this is your life and your journey and you have the power of personal choice. Keep in mind as you face difficult hurdles to always concentrate on your positive qualities. This allows you to discover your personal resources and feel more secure with the decisions you make."

Jasmine's life is chaotic. Her mother is an alcoholic who has been diagnosed with HIV, the virus that leads to AIDS (acquired immuno-deficiency syndrome), which has no cure and eventually leads to death. Out of necessity, Jasmine had to grow up quickly. She always behaved maturely because "someone had to." When Jasmine talks about her ability to hold on, she credits her skills in problem solving, **goal setting**, and finding information so she knew what needed to be done. "Sometimes it was a matter of barely holding on. But I always did," she says.

Jasmine did not always have these skills, but they were what kept her from following in her mother's footsteps. In Werner and Smith's research, they found that the resilient people considered their own personal competence and self-determination to be their best resource for coping. This is true for Jasmine because she has had to dig deep to find and develop the skills to handle her life.

Do you see any similarities between your life and Jasmine's? Maybe school, health, or friends are among your problems. Whatever the difficult situation in your life, problem solving, goal setting, and finding and using information are what you need in order to take control and build the life you want.

Let's face it. Everyone has problems, right? Although problems are certainly not any fun, it is how you manage them that makes the difference between experiencing a minor blip in your life and a major catastrophe.

Sometimes people procrastinate and problems grow. They waste time worrying about the problem rather than solving it. Problems are like quicksand. When handled poorly, they can overwhelm you and suck you under.

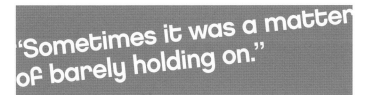

"Sometimes it was a matter of barely holding on."

Take a Deep Breath

Did you know that one of the first steps to solving a problem is as simple as taking a deep breath? More than any other organ in the body, your brain needs a steady supply of oxygen. When you're uptight and stressed, you tend to breathe shallowly. When this happens, your brain doesn't get enough oxygen and you feel mentally sluggish.

Hold your breath for a count of five

1, 2, 3, 4, 5. . .

So what should you do when faced with a major decision? First, relax. Second, breathe deeply. Relax your shoulders, upper chest, and stomach muscles, allowing your diaphragm to move down as you breathe in through your nose. Hold your breath for a count of five, then slowly exhale through your mouth. Learning to breathe correctly might take some practice, but it will help you become a better problem solver.

Problems come in all shapes and sizes. Some problems are personal; some occur because of conflicting values. Some happen because hey, life isn't fair or easy! Author M. Scott Peck spells it out clearly in his book *The Road Less Traveled*, when he says, "Life is difficult. Life is a series of problems. Do we want to moan about them or solve them?"

The good news about problems is that you can learn how to solve them. One of the best ways to approach a problem was created by Dr. Gregory Williams, professor of special education at Pacific Lutheran University in Tacoma, Washington. He calls it the ICAN process.

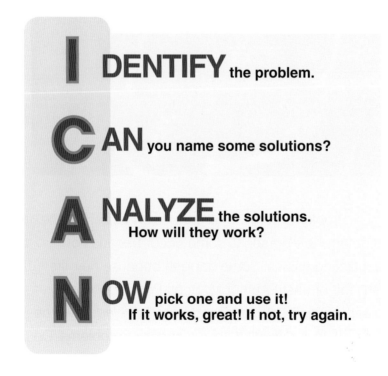

IDENTIFY the problem.

CAN you name some solutions?

ANALYZE the solutions. How will they work?

NOW pick one and use it! If it works, great! If not, try again.

ICAN Work It Out!

Let's take a look at the ICAN process in action: Matt has been invited to a party Saturday night. All his friends will be there, a band has been hired to play, and he has heard there will be a keg of beer. Matt has a dilemma. He wants to go to the party, but as student council president, he knows that if the party gets busted by the police, he will be in big trouble. In order to participate in sports or clubs, students at his school must sign a pledge not to use drugs or alcohol on or off campus. If he gets caught, Matt will lose his student council position, and he doesn't want that to happen.

Matt has a DILEMMA

First, Matt has to **IDENTIFY** the problem. You have to understand it before you can begin to solve it. It can be harder than you think to identify the real problem as opposed to what comes to mind first. It requires reflection and thought. Try any of the following, to help you focus:

- If you like to talk, find friends or adults you trust.
- If you like to write, organize your thoughts in a journal. After a few days, you can reread what you have written, which helps put the problem into perspective.
- If you like to move, take a walk or jog around the neighborhood.
- If you like to listen, put on some music and sing about the problem.

Another way to help you identify the problem is to ask the important questions: who, what, where, when, why, and how.

WHAT'S YOUR problem?

Questions You Can Ask Yourself

WHO is involved in the problem/ knows about the problem/has been through a similar problem?

WHAT can I do now to solve the problem?

WHERE did the problem occur?

HOW have I tried to solve the problem?

Now let's apply the **ICAN** process to Matt's problem.

IDENTIFY the problem

Matt signed a pledge that he wouldn't drink alcohol while serving as student council president. If he gets caught, he will lose that position.

CAN you name some solutions?

This requires some real **brainstorming**; the more options, the better. When Matt brainstorms, he comes up with these choices. He could

- go to the party;
- invite some friends over instead of going to the party;
- tell his friends he is not willing to risk losing the student council position;
- tell his friends he has been grounded so he can't go to the party.

A NALYZE the solutions

Here Matt discards options that are completely untrue or unrealistic. Finally, he comes down to two possibilities: either go to the party, or tell his friends he is not willing to take the risk.

N OW pick a solution

Now it is time to choose an option and stick to it. Matt decides he is not willing to chance being at the party, so he tells his close friends that he isn't going to risk losing his student council presidency and will stay home.

Stay Home

GO

Is this what you would have chosen? Maybe not, but it works for Matt. If you decide to use the ICAN process, write down each step. After a while, it will all just come to you naturally.

ICAN is a great strategy for identifying and setting goals, but there are other ways for you to learn how to solve problems. One is called **FLIP it!** It was developed by Alice Yucht, a school librarian in New Jersey. She wanted to help students find information to use in school assignments. She created this five-step process not only for school assignments but also to help solve personal problems and set goals.

Here is how it works

FLIP it!

FOCUS on your topic or problem.

LOCATE the appropriate resources you need to solve the problem.

INVESTIGATE and implement the information you have discovered.

PRODUCE the results of your findings in an assignment or a solution.

it! Evaluate what you have found by using "Intelligent Thinking" and asking If/Then questions such as "**IF** I want to go to college, **THEN** I need to take the required sequence of courses."

Source: www.aliceinfo.org

FLIP it! can also be described like this:

 **1** Identify the problem because information is key. Understand what needs to be done and ask yourself: What do I really need to do? What do I need to find out?

2 Brainstorm so you know the best resource to use. Is it a book, an Internet site, a person?

 **3** Skim/read/listen to the information to make sure it addresses the problem at hand.

4 Use the information to solve the problem.

 **5** Evaluate the information. Do you need more? Is the problem solved? If not, you need to keep searching.

Let's see this process at work. Remember Jasmine and her concern about her alcoholic mother? Here is how **FLIP it!** could help her.

F

Jasmine is determined not to follow in her mother's footsteps and decides the best way to do that is to learn more about alcoholism.

L

Jasmine asks school and public librarians to show her how to use the online catalog find books and search databases for up-to-date information on alcoholism. She learns how to use the best keywords and look through the phone book to find helpful mental health organizations.

I

Jasmine searches the library for books and articles about whether children of alcoholics are more likely to suffer from the disease. She skims them, carefully reading the titles, subheadings, picture captions, and graphs before she decides if this information will help her learn about alcoholism.

P

Jasmine copies several articles to read later and puts each in a file she has started about children of alcoholics.

it!

Jasmine reflects on her resources about children of alcoholics. She feels confident that the information she has found will help her explain her fears and concerns to a responsible adult, such as a counselor or therapist, who can help guide her as she pursues her goal of avoiding her mother's bad decisions.

SETTING GOALS is sort of like planning a road trip. It helps to think ahead and plan what you need to do to achieve your goal.

Do you have a dream? Do you know what you want out of life? Do you want to get good grades, be popular, or become famous? Why do the dreams of some people come true, while the dreams of others do not? The difference is hard work and goal setting. Think of goal setting as a road trip. Like a journey, goals can be short and quick or long and distant. Once the destination (the goal) of the trip has been determined, the map (the goal-setting plan) helps you follow the most direct route to the final destination. In between is lots of driving (hard work). To help reach your goal, you can use the **ICAN** or **FLIP it!** processes in the same way you would to solve a problem.

Many areas in your life can benefit from goals. They don't just happen on their own, though. You have to put a plan in motion to help them happen.

STEP
1

IDENTIFY YOUR GOAL.
Write it down. Put it in positive terms such as "I will study two hours every night so I can get an A in biology," not "I'll try not to fail biology." Be as specific as possible.

STEP
2

BRAINSTORM WAYS TO ACHIEVE YOUR GOAL.
Try doing it with friends or a trusted adult if possible. When you brainstorm, think of as many ways as possible to achieve your goal. It might help to read about people who have reached their goals to understand how they did it.

"Our greatest glory is not in never falling, but in rising every time we fall."
— Confucius

"When I look at the kids training today … I can tell which ones are going to do well. It's not necessarily the ones who have the most natural talent or who fall the least. Sometimes it's the kids who fall the most, and keep pulling themselves up and trying again."

—Michelle Kwan, figure skater and Olympic medalist

STEP
3

ANALYZE THE IDEAS YOU HAVE BRAINSTORMED.
Which of these ideas appeals to you the most? To better understand your goal, you might want to read more about it.

STEP
4

IT'S TIME FOR ACTION— GO FOR IT!
This is the most important part because it separates the dreamers from the doers. A dream is a desire, but a goal is something you are willing to work for.

In this chapter, you have seen how kids can use systems like **ICAN** and **FLIP it!** to achieve goals, find out information, and gain resiliency in their lives. These are skills that anyone can use in any challenging situation.

But What About my problems?

Take a moment and think about problems you may be facing right now and ask yourself these questions:

- **Can you see how one or both of these processes might help you figure out what to do next?**

- **How can these systems help you to find potential solutions?**

- **What resources might help you make progress?**

- **Do you have goals that you want to achieve? What actions do you need to take in order to activate them?**

test your
goal-setting IQ
Look over the following questions. What words fit the blanks best? Do you know? If not, go back and reread the information you need so that you have a better understanding.

1. _____ is the process of thinking of as many ideas, options, and possibilities as I can.
   - a. journaling
   - b. daydreaming
   - c. brainstorming
   - d. researching

2. Putting things off until the very last minute is an example of _____, and it can sabotage goals.
   - a. visualization
   - b. acceleration
   - c. prioritization
   - d. procrastination

3. One way to wake up your brain is to make sure you _____ carefully and deeply.
   - a. stretch
   - b. breathe
   - c. sleep
   - d. concentrate

4. Options must be both _____ and under your _____.
   - a. realistic; control
   - b. ambitious; skill level
   - c. aggressive; wing
   - d. easy; breath

5. The "it" in FLIP it! stands for _____ _____ and _____ questions.
   - a. information technology; Internet/technical
   - b. immediate talking; instant/timely
   - c. in theory; itemized/tallied
   - d. intelligent thinking; if/then

6. You should always phrase your goals in _____ terms.
   - a. simple
   - b. cautious
   - c. positive
   - d. complex

Answer key: (1) c.; (2) d.; (3) b.; (4) a.; (5) d.; (6) c.

chapter three

Ariel, 14

the human
touch

the human touch

"ASK YOURSELF WHAT IS IMPORTANT TO YOU . . ."

Ariel's Story

Ariel, 14, came home to her father's shocking announcement that her family was moving. "I totally freaked out," she admits. "I don't think he realizes how hard this will be for me."

Moving is extremely stressful, but Dr. Scott has a few suggestions. "Ask yourself what is important to you about fitting in to this new place. More than likely it's making friends and being liked. The best way," says Scott, "is to build your own **self-esteem** by thinking positive thoughts about yourself and being true to your values and beliefs. Most importantly, give yourself time to adjust to all these changes."

Who's Got Skills?

Social skills are the skills that will allow you to adjust to new and challenging situations such as moving. Teens who have good social skills are often better at finding the resources they need to cope with stress through the relationships they form. They know how to make and keep friends. They can be assertive without being aggressive. They can resolve anger without becoming violent and fighting. They also have empathy, a social skill that helps people understand the feelings of others. They are helpful and communicate effectively.

Nothing is as overwhelming as feeling alone in the face of adversity. Not only can your friends help you out in a pinch, but they can listen to your feelings about what's going on in your life. Talking about your problems helps put them into perspective, whether or not your friends can relate to what you're going through. Also, your friends may know of resources, such as a counselor who gives good advice, that you didn't know were available to you.

Do you have a lot of friends?

Have you ever wondered why or why not?

Here are the five **MOST** liked qualities in others. How do you do in each department?
- a sense of humor
- friendliness
- helpfulness
- complimenting others
- extending offers to get together

Can you guess what the five **LEAST** liked qualities are? Do you see yourself in here?
- yelling and using inappropriate language
- anger
- dishonesty
- being critical
- bossiness

Listen Up!

Making friends takes a lot of different skills. One of them is simply being a good conversationalist. Does that mean you are a good talker? No. It's more about being a good listener. How can you do that?

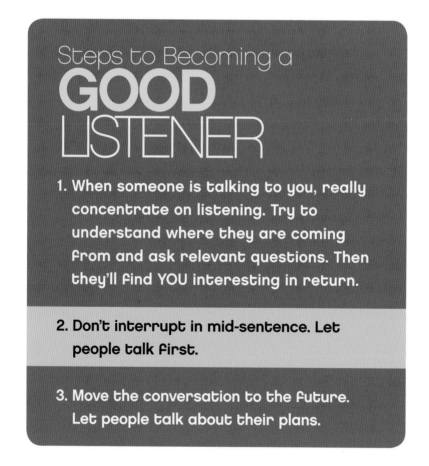

Steps to Becoming a
GOOD
LISTENER

1. **When someone is talking to you, really concentrate on listening. Try to understand where they are coming from and ask relevant questions. Then they'll find YOU interesting in return.**

2. **Don't interrupt in mid-sentence. Let people talk first.**

3. **Move the conversation to the future. Let people talk about their plans.**

Do You See What I'm Saying?

Having strong social skills goes way beyond carrying on conversations in the lunch line. It's also being able to use and understand nonverbal cues such as facial expressions, posture, and gestures. It's important to be able to "read" these nonverbal cues because anywhere from 65 to 90 percent of the emotional meaning of a message is communicated this way.

Has someone ever told you something and the words they used said one thing, but their nonverbal cues indicated the exact opposite? Your friend tells you he's interested in what you're saying, but he's looking at a magazine and sits slumped in his chair. His body language is telling you that he's bored. The true meaning of the message is more likely found in the nonverbal cues.

No really, I'm listening.

Nonverbal cues tell you a lot about what people mean—all without saying a single word. They include:

facial expressions: The look on a person's face often lets you know what he or she is thinking and feeling.

eye contact: The old expression states that the eyes are the window to the soul. They can reveal what a person is thinking.

body language: The way people stand, walk, and sit lets others know a lot about what they are thinking and feeling. For example, crossed arms can indicate they don't believe what they are hearing.

gestures: Arm, hand, and head movements can give you an insight into people's personalities. If they make a lot of gestures while talking, they appear passionate and energetic. If they're motionless while speaking, it can mean they are bored.

paralinguistics: This means how words sound when they come out of someone's mouth. The pitch, tone, loudness, rhythm, and emphasis all carry meaning.

Unspoken Rules

Do you think it is easy to understand nonverbal cues? It isn't. There are actually rules to figuring them out, but learning them can be challenging. These rules are not written down anywhere. They are often learned in a very haphazard fashion. You might have picked them up from your parents or from watching your friends.

It is important to avoid breaking the rules of nonverbal cues because if you don't, the conflicts and confrontations that can arise can be extremely stressful and difficult to deal with. It has happened to almost everyone. Have you noticed how people react if you stand too close to them in line? What happens if you stare at someone too long? The person usually begins to fidget and get uncomfortable and may look or move away. This is a big sign that

a noneverbal-cue rule has just been broken!

Work It Out

Regardless of how great your social skills are, misunderstandings and conflicts still occur with your family and friends. What do you do when this happens? The most important step is to stay calm and relax. Take some of those deep breaths. Count to ten. Take a walk. Write in your journal. Then, once emotions are under control, you can work to resolve conflicts through a modified version of the FLIP it! process.

Use **FLIP it!** if you are angry:

FOCUS on the cause. What triggered the argument?

LOOK at the other person's point of view objectively.

IDENTIFY what you both agree on.

PLAN a mutually agreeable way to resolve the problem. If you can't agree on something, then agree to disagree and to stop fighting!

it! Did you solve the conflict? **IF NOT, THEN WHAT** do you both need to do to have peace?

The Power of a Mentor

Oprah Winfrey had one. So did Tom Brokaw, a well-respected NBC television anchor, and Lynn Swann, an all-time record holder for the Pittsburgh Steelers football team. What did they have? A **mentor**.

MENTOR any caring adult who makes an active, positive contribution to the life of a child who is not his or her own; someone who has found ways to succeed in life and cares enough to pass those lessons along

People who are successful in life often remember a special person—a mentor—who helped them become a better person. It is little surprise then that the most important protective factor for resiliency is mentoring. The purpose of a mentor is to provide guidance, support, reassurance, friendship, and perspective to a young person. Although friends can offer support, there is something special about connecting with someone who is older and more experienced.

MENTOR

RESILIENT?

Mentoring helps teens to:

grow up

A mentor helps teens learn what it takes to become a responsible and successful adult. It helps to get an adult's perspective on challenges you are facing.

make decisions

In the journey toward adulthood, it is important to learn how to make good decisions. However, sometimes you make mistakes. It is easier to learn from them when there is a caring adult to help you understand what went wrong and what to do differently next time.

set goals

A mentor helps teens focus on important pursuits.

have fun

Growing up can be a struggle, and it is easy to forget to have fun. Mentors can give emotional support and help teens find time for fun.

Do you have someone in your life who is like a mentor to you? Mentors can make a big difference. The research proves it. For example, one study revealed that youth mentored by Big Brothers/Big Sisters volunteers were less likely to use drugs and alcohol and skip school. Mentees (those who are mentored) generally feel more positive about school, the future, and helping others.

Finding a Mentor

There are two kinds of mentoring relationships, although their benefits and purposes are the same. The first type is informal. These mentors are people you already know, such as grandparents, neighbors, adult friends of the family, teachers, or ministers. In an informal mentoring relationship, you and the mentor already know each other and decide—often without saying a thing—what the relationship will be like.

The second type of mentoring is formal. Here an organization brings together teens with volunteers who have been trained in mentoring. The organization introduces them to each other, provides training, and sets rules about how often to meet and for how long. You can find these organizations on the Internet or in a phone book. You can also ask a librarian, teacher, or guidance counselor.

Formal Mentoring Organizations

Big Brothers/Big Sisters
Boys and Girls Clubs of America
Boy Scouts of America
Girl Scouts of the USA
YMCA/YWCA

If you are looking for an informal mentor, there are several steps to finding one.

Understand the reasons you want a mentor. Do you need help with homework? Do you need a sympathetic ear? Do you want someone to help you explore careers?

Make a list of the people you know who might be mentor candidates. Whittle it down by asking these important questions: Do I like this person? Can we have fun? Will I be able to discuss my life with him or her? Is this person a good role model? Does this person have time to spend with me?

Meet with a potential mentor to discuss the mentoring relationship. You must be able to tell this person what you want from a mentor and why you think he or she would be a good one. Now go ahead and ask this person to be your mentor! If he or she is unable to become your mentor because of family or work responsibilities, don't feel rejected. Keep looking. Maybe this person can help you find a mentor.

Time to Volunteer

Have you ever thought about sharing your time, energy, and enthusiasm by helping others? According to researchers, about thirteen million teens spend two to three hours each week volunteering. Why would a busy teen volunteer? It's simple—the rewards are enormous! Studies show that teens who volunteer just two hours per week have higher self-esteem and more resilience. They learn how to set and reach goals and they have more confidence in their decisions. Teens who volunteer are 50 percent less likely to smoke, drink, or use drugs. Also, a more professional environment can expose a teen to productive ways in which people can cope with stress.

VOLUNTEER= REWARDS

Although teens who volunteer do not receive a paycheck to cash at the bank, they realize volunteering is a win-win situation for them, the organization, or the individuals receiving help.

volunteering
Can Help YOU

- meet new people;
- gain experiences helpful to your future career goals;
- learn about an activity that interests you;
- develop leadership skills;
- build a resume;
- show employers you are responsible;
- obtain letters of recommendation;
- build confidence in your abilities;
- learn new ways to solve problems;
- develop goal-setting skills, such as how to prioritize;
- learn to work with other people;
- understand the needs of others.

Serious Rewards

Do you know what the MOST important benefit of volunteering is? It's the GREAT feeling you get when you care about other people. Teens who volunteer develop **empathy**, or the ability to care for and understand the feelings of another person. Teens who volunteer focus less on themselves and their own problems and become more aware of the challenges others face. You can learn a lot from other peoples' experiences and how they have dealt with the challenges in their lives.

If you volunteer, you need to take it seriously. The services you perform are important to the organization or individual helped, even though there aren't any paychecks involved. People are counting on you. Show up when you are scheduled, dress appropriately, and perform the job with creativity, care, and diligence.

"Life's most urgent question is: What are you doing for others?"

Martin Luther King Jr.

Just like mentoring, there are informal and formal ways to volunteer. Informal volunteer opportunities can be found within your neighborhood and community. Ask yourself: Does the elderly couple next door need help shoveling snow in the winter? Could the frazzled mom next door use a free babysitter? Does my library need help with the summer reading program? Would the neighborhood look better if I picked up trash?

There are also many, many formal opportunities to volunteer. Check out your YMCA/ YWCA, the Red Cross, public libraries, animal shelters, food banks, and hospitals. Call them and ask about volunteer needs. Many organizations have volunteer coordinators who can answer your questions. Although every organization hires its volunteers differently, you will most likely be asked about your skills and how you think you can best help. You might even receive training to help you become a better volunteer.

Back to Ariel's Story

Rember Ariel from the beginning of the chapter? After Ariel's father surprised her with the news that the family was moving, she was miserable. Her first response was to write in her journal and pour out her thoughts and feelings. Every few days she would reread what she had written. By reflecting on her words she came to realize that the move was going to happen and she might as well make the best of it. She realized that if she sulked and acted miserable, she would only be hurting herself because who wants to be with someone acting sad and angry? First, she accepted the situation, then she started to make a plan.

Ariel realized that many of the good times she had at school were because of her friends. Ariel decided to concentrate on meeting people and making friends. She made a point of talking to teachers who might help her get involved with clubs. These teachers became mentors for her. She was kind to people in her community by becoming a volunteer at a nursing home. Ariel was able to become more resilient and make the best of a move to a new place by making friends, finding adults to mentor her, and helping people in need.

Some teens find that keeping a journal helps them cope with stress.

Do You Have the
humantouch?

Test what you've learned about how relationships with others help you become more resilient.

1. Which of the following is one of the most liked qualities in others?
   - a. good looks
   - b. helpful to others
   - c. responsible behaviors
   - d. generous with gifts

2. Making friends helps you become more resilient by:
   - a. providing more opportunities to receive gifts.
   - b. having people to gossip with.
   - c. providing a support network for times of need.
   - d. telling other people what to do.

3. Which of the following is NOT a nonverbal cue?
   - a. crossing your arms
   - b. introducing yourself
   - c. winking
   - d. nodding your head

4. Mentoring can help you do which of the following?
   - a. make money
   - b. avoid your homework
   - c. stay up later
   - d. have fun

5. Which of the following is NOT a way volunteering can help you become more resilient?
   - a. get better grades
   - b. find people with common interests
   - c. learn to be a leader
   - d. gain confidence in your decisions

Answer key: (1) b.; (2) c.; (3) b.; (4) d.; (5) a.

friendship

can definitely help you deal with the stress you face everyday.

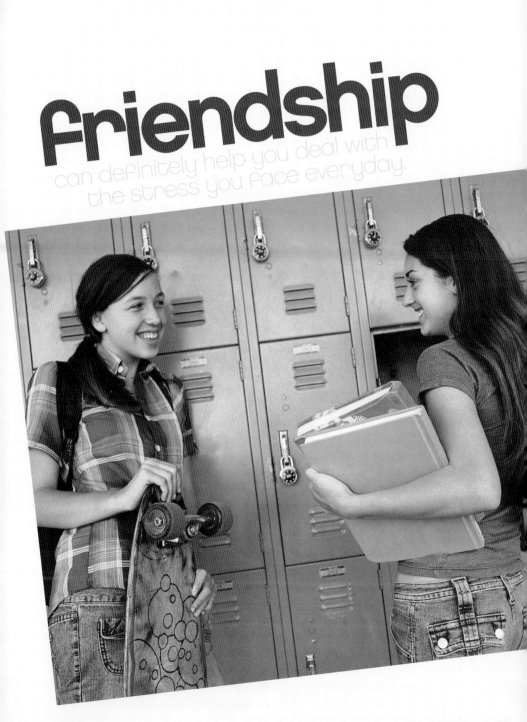

chapter four

Greg, 17

flexing
muscles,
mind and
spirit

"... RESIST NEGATIVE PEER PRESSURE"

Greg's Story

Greg, 17, is faced with a problem he does not know how to deal with. "Most of my friends think I have a great life—and I really do," he states. "My problem is that my parents are gone all the time. They own a restaurant, and they work crazy hours. I want to spend more time with them. I am an only child, and I get lonely."

At one time or another, every person winds up in a difficult situation. The most resilient teens are the ones who know how to comfort themselves and find the right protective factors to meet their needs.

Hobbies, Activities, and Sports

What do running on the school's track team, playing the guitar, and writing poetry all have in common? For some teens, these are simply fun ways to spend time. For struggling teens, however, hobbies, activities, and sports can help you cope with stress because they

- act as a decoy to take your mind off the negative things happening in life;
- help you feel less stressed because you are enjoying yourself;
- boost self-esteem because you are involved in an activity that you value and are probably pretty good at;
- are a great way to meet new people and make friends.

If you don't have a **hobby** or activity that you enjoy, it's a great time to start. You can even apply the ICAN process to help you.

Using **ICAN** to Find Hobbies, Activities, and Sports:

IDENTIFY **hobbies, activities, and sports that interest you.**

CAN **you brainstorm ways to learn about them?**

ANALYZE **what you have come up with and make plans to learn about and add hobbies, activities, and sports to your life.**

NOW **start having fun!**

Just as you did in the other chapter, work through each step of the ICAN process.

ICAN Find a Way to be More Active!

Think about all of the different hobbies, activities, and sports that you find appealing. They can be individual (tennis, skateboarding) or team sports (football, basketball), artistic (painting, photography), or crafty (scrapbooking, calligraphy).

Brainstorm ways to learn about these activities. Ask the question, "How can I learn more about these hobbies?" Perhaps you can learn about it through the Internet or reading books or magazines at the public library or bookstore. Ask, "Do I need to take lessons?" If the answer is yes, identify organizations or businesses that provide instruction. Oftentimes, low-cost instruction is available at community centers, the YMCA or YWCA, public libraries, or even your school. Ask others about their hobbies. Why do you enjoy it? How do you learn more about it? How much do supplies and equipment cost?

3 Analyze what you have learned. If you are still excited about the activity, come up with a plan to start it. Sign up for lessons or purchase supplies.

4 This one is the easiest! Just start having fun with your new activity!

The Power of Pursuits

Good health is an important protective factor, but you can't control the genes you inherited. The truth is, the more problems and challenges you face, the more protective factors and developmental assets you will need.

Mattie Stepanek was born with a rare genetic disorder called mitochondrial myopathy, which interferes with the regulation of automatic body functions such as breathing, the beating of the heart, blood pressure, body temperature, and digestion. A ventilator helped him breathe. A second machine pumped medicines and intravenous fluids directly into his heart. He underwent weekly blood transfusions.

Mattie Stepanek

Despite all of this, Mattie never let health problems keep him from enjoying life. Creative writing was a favorite way for him to cope with health problems. Starting at the age of three, he expressed his message about hope and peace in poems, short stories, and essays. His writing was so well received that five of his books became best sellers. Mattie also enjoyed hobbies such as building with LEGO bricks, reading, rock collecting, and chess.

As spokesperson for the Muscular Dystrophy Association, Mattie was able to reach out to kids all over the world facing the hardships of living with chronic disease before he died on June 22, 2004, just three weeks before his 14th birthday.

Kids living with chronic disease may have to work harder at developing resiliency, but the rewards of their hard work remind the world of the power of positive thinking.

Time to Read

Do you like to read? If so, you aren't alone. According to an online survey conducted by SmartGirl.com and the American Library Association, 72 percent of teens like to read for pleasure. The number-one problem with reading for fun is finding the time for it. It is an important hobby to find time for, however. It is not only educational but also another one of those important protective factors.

How can reading help you to be more resilient? Reading is a terrific way to at least temporarily escape from difficulties in life. Unlike drugs and alcohol, reading is a healthy way to take your mind off of your troubles.

RESILIENT **TEENS**

know how to put distance between themselves and their troubles.

Reading for pleasure can help you become a better reader and, in turn, a better student. All teens need to read, not just to get through school but to gather information to improve life, make decisions, set goals, and have fun.

Every year, more than **A MILLION TEENS DROP OUT OF HIGH SCHOOL**—often because they can't read.

Why do some teens refuse to read? It could be that they are simply not strong readers. For them, reading isn't relaxing—it's a struggle. Another reason teens may avoid reading is that it seems **B-O-R-I-N-G**. There is often so much emphasis on reading material for class, which they don't enjoy, that they make the assumption that all reading is dull.

feed
your head!

Not sure how to start looking for something to read? Ask yourself these quesions:

- What am I interested in?
- What do I want to know more about?
- What TV shows/movies intrigue me?
- What skill do I want to learn?
- What did I just hear about at school/in the news that was interesting?
- What kind of people do I want to learn more about?
- What kind of job do I see myself in?

Don't let yourself get caught in the trap that if you are going to read, it has to be a 1,000-page book. It can be a magazine, a Web site, a comicbook, a graphic novel, or a newspaper. Check with your local library and bookstores. Try just scanning titles and see which one grabs your attention.

Ask your friends, too. See if they have read something great that they can recommend. You can solve mysteries, follow the trail of real criminals, or learn a new hobby. Magazine articles can keep you up-to-date on your favorite sports team or the hottest music group. You can find out how to make pizza or how to drop the engine out of a 1974 Volkswagen Beetle. There really is something out there for everyone if you just take the time to look for it.

Spirituality, Faith, and Religion

Who am I? What happens to my body and spirit when I die? Is there a God? These questions are asked by all people at one time or another. It is only natural to search for meaning in life. Teens are especially interested in asking these questions and searching for answers to help them figure out who they are and how to live. It's important to understand your place in the world. What you believe can and does change and evolve over time as you experience different things and make new friends. You may find as you grow that your beliefs may be different from those of other family members and friends.

The terms *spirituality*, *faith*, and *religion* are often used to mean the same thing. Each one has a slightly different meaning, though.

spirituality—the personal search for meaning, wholeness, and purpose in life; it is a broad concept that may not have anything to do with religion

faith—how you show loyalty to a cause, person, or belief in a higher being

religion—your allegiance to a particular system of faith and worship, of which there are many

majorreligions **of the World**

- **Bahaism**
- **Buddhism**
- **Catholicism**
- **Christianity**
- **Confucianism**
- **Hinduism**
- **Islam**

- **Judaism**
- **Mormonism**
- **Religious Society of Friends/Quakers**
- **Sikhism**
- **Taoism**
- **Unitarianism**

For many teens, spirituality, faith, and religion are all positive and important parts of life—especially when their beliefs help them become stronger and more resilient.

Facts about teens and RELIGION

- **Teens who have strong belief systems are less likely to engage in unsafe sex, use illegal drugs and alcohol, or commit suicide.**

- **Religious twelfth graders in the United States are more positive about life than their less-religious peers.**

- **Thirty percent of high school seniors say religion is very important to them.**

Source: Smith, Christian and Robert Faris. "Religion and the Life Attitudes and Self Images of American Adolescents." *A Research Study of the National Study of Life and Religion Number 2*, December 2002.

Why are spirituality, faith, and religion beneficial? They often lead to improved physical and emotional health because many belief systems encourage moderation and healthy living. Teens who attend religious services often have better grades and school attendance because religious communities tend to teach and reinforce behaviors such as concern for others, empathy, and responsible actions. Religious teens also tend to believe that if they need help, people in their religious community will be there to offer it.

In addition to being good for finding mentors and helpful services, places of worship are also good for teens, according to the Search Institute, because they

- help reduce risky behaviors;
- teach values;
- welcome people of all ages;
- provide caring and support;
- have high expectations for teens;
- provide opportunities to become involved;
- encourage service to others;
- nurture social skills and leadership;
- offer security and stability.

Get Up, Get Out, and Do Something!

Joining a religious group is not the only way to become part of a community. For many teens, non-religious groups that work within their community provide the same kind of support network and spiritual gratification that they need for staying resilient. Perhaps you are passionate about the environment. You can look into groups that are active in making your community—and your world—a better place to live, from cleaning up public spaces to educating companies on better ways to operate responsibly.

Many cities and towns offer programs for kids and teens that provide activities, or simply spaces to hang out in, that you can become part of. After-school programs and groups that meet on the weekends can be great resources in finding new people to connect with as well as new activities that you may enjoy. Check in at your local library, museums, or community center and see what they have to offer. You might be surprised at how many choices you have when it comes to finding a group to become part of.

Back to Greg's Story

Remember Greg from the beginning of the chapter? He feels left out in his family's busy schedule. Do you ever wish you could spend more time with your family? A close bond with your family is an important protective factor when coping with stress. However, often the realities of family life, such as work or divorce, don't allow kids to spend as much time with their parents as they would like. So what can kids like Greg do to ensure that they will still have the personal resources necessary to deal with life's pressures?

In situations like Greg's, you need to relax and have some "ME" time. In their research, Dr. Emmy Werner and Ruth Smith discovered that the most resilient teens were able to self-comfort. What does this mean? It is important to develop healthy habits and recharge physically, mentally, and spiritually.

"To move ahead you need to believe in yourself. . . . Have conviction in your beliefs and the confidence to execute those beliefs."

—Adlin Sinclair, a British motivational speaker and humanitarian

Advice for Greg

Greg needs to set some goals for dealing with his dilemma. He needs to find a way to feel more connected with his over-worked parents and he needs to find other sources of strength that he can draw upon in times of need. Dr. Scott has two pieces of advice for Greg:

1 It's pretty easy to feel rejected when we have expectations for relationships—whether with parents or friends—that are seldom met. Frequently, this is the result of poor communication. Tell your parents what you want. Let them know how much they mean to you and that you want more time with them. Together you can brainstorm ways to get more involved in each other's schedules.

2 Look for opportunities to get involved in activities that help you feel successful and connected to people. You can do this by becoming active in your community—by joining a youth group at church, developing hobbies, learning a new sport, getting involved in school activities, or volunteering at a local food bank or homeless shelter. Whatever your interests, be sure to act on them. Take control of your life so you will feel good about it.

resiliency fitness

_____ 1. Hobbies are things teens do because they are required to by family, friends, or teachers.

_____ 2. The ICAN process can be used to identify which hobbies fit me the best.

_____ 3. Going online can connect me with a great deal of the information I need to become resilient.

_____ 4. One of the main reasons kids do not like to read is because they think most books are boring.

_____ 5. Illiteracy can lead to much bigger problems later in life.

_____ 6. Books are the only kind of reading material that is truly educational.

_____ 7. Spirituality, faith, and religion are synonyms; they all mean the exact same thing.

_____ 8. Joining a religious group is the only way to get involved in your community.

Answer key: (1) False; (2) True; (3) True; (4) True; (5) True; (6) False; (7) False; (8) False

chapter five

Maria, 16

ICAN become more resilient

"LIFE IS A BALANCING ACT . . ."

Maria's Story

Like many kids, Maria, 16, has faced problems similar to those described in this book. "How do I make a plan right now to become more resilient?" she asks. "Can you tell me the most important protective factors to add to my life?"

Maria's question is an excellent one. As Dr. Scott says, "Life is a balancing act, and it is natural to experience both good times and bad. When you're experiencing challenges, it is important that you take the initiative and add good things like protective factors to your life. They are like Teflon because they can form an invisible shield to keep life's adversities from sticking to us."

Mnemonic—used as an aid in remembering

How can you add these factors to your own life? Dr. Scott recommends a simple process called MORALITY as an easy-to-remember mnemonic device.

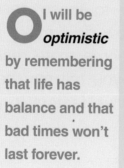

M I will *motivate* myself to stay healthy and resist being dragged down by the negative.

O I will be *optimistic* by remembering that life has balance and that bad times won't last forever.

R I will build *relationships* by surrounding myself with people who want the best for me.

A I will *act* to become resilient, beginning today.

This book can help you develop your plan to add protective factors that lead to resilience. To start, use the ICAN process to develop a resiliency plan.

I **DENTIFY** your goal. Your goal: to become more resilient.

C **REATE**/brainstorm steps to add protective factors to your life.

A **NALYZE** the steps and develop a plan.

N **OW** go for it! The most important step is to put your plan into motion.

L I will *laugh* at adversity because a sense of humor will help me put life's ups and downs into perspective.

I will celebrate my *individualism* by believing that "I'm worth it and I can achieve my dreams and goals."

T I will *trust* in myself and know I am in control.

Y *Yes*, I am able to face anything and succeed.

The Art of Making Good Choices

Can you remember times when you made the WRONG choice about something? Usually the fallout is not fun to deal with. Making good choices is a skill that depends on your ability to solve problems, set goals to get where you want to go, and use information so decisions are based on knowledge and facts, not ignorance. The following activities can help you.

GETTING TO KNOW
yourself

1 Understanding yourself is a first step in deciding what is important to you and what you want from life. No one can answer these questions for you because you are unique and so is your life! Take the fun and free online tests at http://queendom.com. You can find out a lot about yourself, from if your personality is "normal" to what career might be best for you. At http://similarminds.com/personality_tests.html, you can find out even more, including whether you are dominated by the right or left side of your brain.

2 If you don't already have a journal, start one now. Try to write every day. Reflecting on your life and the decisions you have made will help put your life into perspective. A great place to start is Journal Tips at http://journal.lifetips.com/cat/59631/journaling-for-teens/.

3 Develop your decision-making skills by dissecting a decision that was made by someone you know or even a fictional character in a book. Use the ICAN process to understand the why, what, and how of the decision. If it turned out badly, don't gloat. We all make decisions at one time or another that don't turn out as we expect. The important thing to do is to understand the decision-making process and why some decisions work out and others don't.

REFLECT
on your life

October 11, 2006

My worst habit:
PROCRASTINATION

4 Look at the HOT site (an Oakland, California, project that teaches teens about HIV/AIDS) at www.caps. ucsf.edu/hotdecision.html. Read one of the "Sticky Situations" near the bottom of the page. What would you decide?

5 Before you turn in for the night, take a few minutes to reflect on three good things that happened to you today.

6 Everyone has one or two self-defeating habits—such as telling white lies, procrastinating, or responding with anger—that stand in the way of reaching a goal. Identify a bad habit of yours and brainstorm ways to overcome it. Then develop an action plan. Start with what you will do tomorrow and identify the date you will overcome the bad habit.

7 Take time to reflect on these questions: What are my boundaries? What do I value in life? What are my core beliefs? This may take some profound thought, but knowing the answers will help you make the right decisions in life.

GETTING TO
Know Others

As you learned in chapter 3, teens who have social skills and can empathize with others will have an easier time making friends and communicating with others, whether it's at school, church, or on the job. People who hire employees say the traits most in demand are social skills. You can develop these by being aware of what you say and how you say it, by reaching out to others in need, and by learning how to be a good friend.

Whoopi Goldberg

"When you are kind to someone in trouble, you hope they'll remember and be kind to someone else. And it'll become like wildfire."

8 ways to develope your SOCIAL SKILLS

1. Go to the www.highworld.com/social site and learn more about social skills.

2. Start to use "I sentences" and a technique called active listening. You can learn more about active listening at the Fact Monster site www.factmonster.com/homework/listeningskills1.html.

3. Decide to invite a friend, especially a new one, to go shopping, to a movie, or over to your house this week.

4. Throw a party. Have everyone bring something to eat or drink.

5. Identify organizations in your community that could benefit by having you volunteer. Check out your telephone book's Yellow Pages. Ask at the public library. Call organizations that most interest you and talk to the volunteer coordinator.

6. Read a book or watch a movie about friendship.

7. Consider finding a mentor or becoming one yourself.

8. Start an informal group to welcome new students to your school.

Meeting new people and hanging out with friends is **GOOD FOR YOU!**

Getting Outside Yourself

As you read earlier, sometimes the best way to handle problems is to forget them momentarily by relaxing and doing something you enjoy. You need to find something you like so much that you get totally involved and forget about the stresses and difficulties for a while.

relax
and step outside yourself
Here are some ideas you might try

1 Write a short story and publish it online. Check out this site for ideas: http://teenwriting.about.com/od/placestopublish/.

2 Join a health club or start exercising more. Exercise helps to release serotonin, which is a feel-good hormone produced naturally by your body.

3 Sign up for a class that you know nothing about.

4 Go to the bookstore or library and spend one hour reading and looking through magazines and books you are drawn to.

5 Work on becoming more independent by spending time alone and making it enjoyable.

6 Make a space in your home where you feel comfortable and safe. Keep this space free of clutter and go there when you need to recharge.

7 Attend a religious service, ask people about their place of worship, or talk to people about their faith.

8 List three of your best strengths and three of your worst weaknesses. Use ICAN or FLIP it! to develop the strengths and eliminate the weaknesses.

9 Visualize how you want to live your life. Where do you want to be in five years? Ten years? How do you want people to remember you? When you die, what words do you want written on your tombstone?

Be the Ball

Think back to the bouncing ball we talked about in the beginning. Remember how it is the air inside that gives it the ability to bounce right back, no matter how hard someone throws it? Your ability to bounce back depends on the skills you have learned about in this book. As the people at the resiliency.com site put it, "Resiliency is the ability to spring back from and successfully adapt to adversity. An increasing body of research from the fields of psychology, psychiatry, and sociology is showing that most people—including young people—can bounce back from risks, stress, crises, and trauma and experience life success."

Their favorite definition of resiliency was provided by a 15-year-old high-school student who went through a semester of resiliency training.

"[Resiliency is] bouncing back from problems and stuff with more power and more smarts."

Source: http://resiliency.com/
htm/whatisresiliency.htm

resiliency
CHECKLIST

One of the best Web sites for information about how to become more resilient is the Resiliency Center. It notes that many highly resilient people:

1. Have a playful, childlike curiosity.

These people ask a lot of questions and are endlessly curious about how things work. They play as children do and have a good time almost everywhere they go. They wonder, experiment, make mistakes, laugh, and ask, "What is different now?" "What if I did this?" "Who can answer my questions?"

2. Constantly learn from experience.

These people take in new or unexpected experiences and look for the lessons to be learned. They ask, "What early clues did I ignore?" and reflect on what to do differently next time.

3. Adapt quickly.

Resilient people are emotionally flexible. They exhibit personalities with opposing qualities (i.e., strong and gentle, sensitive and tough, logical and intuitive, calm and emotional, serious and playful, etc.).

4. Have solid self-esteem and self-confidence.

Self-esteem determines how much you learn after something goes wrong. It allows you to receive praise and buffer criticism. Self-confidence allows you to take risks without waiting for the approval of others. You can handle new situations because you have done so in the past.

5. Have good friendships and loving relationships.

Research shows that people who work in negative environments are stronger and more resistant to stress if they have strong relationships with their family and friends. People who tend to keep to themselves are more vulnerable to distressing conditions.

6. Express feelings honestly.

Resilient people can show an entire range of human emotions both honestly and openly. They can also choose to suppress their feelings when they believe it would be best.

7. Expect things to work out well.

These people are optimists with a high tolerance for uncertainty. They can work without a job description and often bring stability to crises and chaos. They seek to handle situations in ways that bring about good results for everyone.

8. Read others with empathy.

Resiliency requires people to see things through the perspectives of others and maintain a win-win attitude in conflicts. They seek to understand how others think and feel.

9. Use intuition, creative hunches.

Resilient people accept their gut feelings as useful sources of information. They pay attention to what their bodies—and even their daydreams—are telling them.

10. Defend self well.

Resiliency means taking care of yourself by being able to fight back and to see through and avoid cons, games, and manipulations that others attempt. Resilient people know how to find the allies, resources, and support they need.

11. Have a talent for serendipity.

Resilient people can convert a situation that is emotionally harmful for others into something emotionally strengthening for them. They gain strength from adversity because they have learned good lessons from bad experiences.

12. Get better and better every decade.

As time goes by, these people become increasingly capable, resilient, playful, and free. They are able to enjoy life more and more.

Source: www.resiliencycenter.
com/articles/resquizscoring.shtml

want to LEARN MORE?

CONTACT **the resiliency center** for more information at:

P.O. Box 535

Portland, OR 97207

503/289-3295

In this chapter, you have been given a lot of possible activities that could bring more resilience into your life. Did any of them jump off the page at you because they sounded like something you would be interested in trying?

As you finish the book, keep these important points in mind:

- **Stress is the problem; resiliency is the solution.**

- **Anyone can learn how to be more resilient in life.**

- **Becoming more self-confident can help you bounce back.**

- **Activities such as volunteering, taking up a new hobby, and journaling are helpful.**

- **You CAN become a more resilient person. Just remember the steps of ICAN and FLIP it!**

what have you
LEARNED?

Remember that quiz you took at the beginning of the book? Here it is again. How would you do on it now? How have your ideas about coping with stress changed?

TRUE or FALSE?

_____ 1. Stress only affects certain people.

_____ 2. The key to coping with stress is to ignore it as much as possible.

_____ 3. Resiliency is the ability to cope with and adapt to the stresses in life.

_____ 4. Some people are just naturally better at coping with stress than others.

_____ 5. Reading is not an effective way of coping with stress.

_____ 6. Volunteering is one way to reduce stress.

_____ 7. Resilient people know how to safely escape from their troubles on a temporary basis.

_____ 8. If you're a person who naturally freaks out from stress, there's very little you can do about it.

Answer key: (1) False; (2) False; (3) True; (4) False; (5) False; (6) True; (7) True; (8) False

adversity—an unfortunate event such as depression, divorce, mental illness, poverty, or parental neglect or abuse that leads to severe problems and challenges

at risk—people who face adversity; are unable to master developmental tasks for their age-group; and are more likely to suffer such things as depression, school failure and dropping out, drug and alcohol abuse, or early sexual experiences that cause additional problems

brainstorming—a technique where you say out loud or write down as many solutions to a problem as possible, no matter how far-fetched, silly, or wild

developmental assets— positive behaviors used when faced with challenges in life; concrete, commonsense, positive experiences and qualities essential to raising successful young people

empathy—the ability to understand the emotions of others, to place oneself in someone else's shoes, and to respond with sensitivity to others; this is the most important social skill

goal setting—the process of identifying goals and working toward achieving them

goals—things to be achieved

high risk—having a greater exposure to problems and challenges

hobby—an activity such as a sport, a craft, or an artistic pursuit that is enjoyed for pleasure or relaxation and not as a main occupation

mentor—a caring adult who makes an active, positive contribution to the life of a child or less experienced person

nonverbal cues—facial expressions, posture, tone of voice, and gestures that help to express meaning without using words

problem-solving—finding the answer to difficulties, uncertainties, and doubt

protective factors—characteristics and qualities that protect individuals from becoming overwhelmed by adversity; protective factors are made up of personal and environmental strengths

self-esteem—a belief in your overall worth and value as a person

social skills—a collection of traits and behaviors that help individuals perform well in social situations

volunteering—giving time to an organization or person without expecting to be paid in return

Books

Espeland, Pamela. *Life Lists for Teens: Tips, Steps, Hints, and How-Tos for Growing Up, Getting Along, Learning, and Having Fun.* Minneapolis: Free Spirit, 2003.

Farrell, Juliana, and Beth Mayall. *Middle School: The Real Deal.* New York: HarperTrophy, 2001.

Gifford, Darcy. *Peace Jam: How Young People Can Make Peace in Their Schools and Communities.* San Francisco: Jossey-Bass, 2004.

Graham, Stedman. *Move without the Ball: Put Your Skills and Your Magic to Work for You.* New York: Simon & Schuster, 2004.

Greene, Rebecca. *The Teenagers' Guide to School Outside the Box.* Minneapolis: Free Spirit, 2001.

Johnson, Spencer. *Who Moved My Cheese? For Teens: An A-Mazing Way to Change and Win!* New York: G. P. Putnam's Sons, 2002.

MacGregor, Cynthia. *Think for Yourself: A Kid's Guide to Solving Life's Dilemmas and Other Sticky Problems.* Montreal: Lobster, 2003.

McGraw, Jay. *Life Strategies for Teens.* New York: Fireside, 2000.

Palmer, Pat, and Melissa Alberti Froehner. *Teen Esteem: A Self-Direction Manual for Young Adults.* 2nd ed. Atascadero, Calif.: Impact Publishers, 2000.

Online Sites & Organizations

Crisis Services
Kids Helpline
2969 Main Street
Buffalo, NY 14214
877/KIDS-400
www.kidscrisis.com

At this Web site, you can
learn more about divorce,
depression, eating disorders,
and self-esteem issues. Join
a chat room, read the Kids
Helpline newsletter, or register
for live chats. If you are having
trouble and need to talk to a
counselor now, the toll-free
helpline is open twenty-four
hours a day.

Journaling for Teens
*journal.lifetips.com/cat/59631/
journaling-for-teens*

A forum for teens to learn new
ideas about keeping a journal.
Rate journal ideas or submit
your own. Follow links to learn
about the many ways journaling
can be part of your life.

Kids 4 Kids
www.kids4kids.com

Founded by Daniela Romano,
and her divorced dad, this Web
site offers teenagers a safe
place to freely express their
feelings regarding divorce,
discuss problems, offer
support, and find hope.

Kids' Turn
1242 Market Street, 2nd Floor
San Francisco, CA 94102-4802
800/392-9239
www.kidsturn.org

A nonprofit organization helping
kids and their families work
through divorce, Kids' Turn
has a Web site that features
activities, artwork, articles, and
frequently asked questions
regarding divorce. Get advice
from professionals and other
teens on how to talk to your
parents about divorce.

About the Author

As a professor and former high school librarian, Jami L. Jones works with educators, librarians, and others to develop skills and programs to help young people cope with the challenges and problems they face. Dr. Jones has established the Amanda Award through the Florida Association of Media in Education, which recognizes school librarians who develop programs that promote self-esteem and resiliency in teens.

Dr. Jones has degrees in sociology and library science and a doctorate in information science. She is an assistant professor in the Department of Library Science and Instructional Technology at East Carolina University in Greenville, North Carolina. She may be contacted through her Helping Teens Cope Web site at www. askdrjami.org.

In writing this book, Dr. Jones consulted Dr. Cindy Crosscope Scott, a psychologist in private practice in Greenville, North Carolina, for her expertise. She has a PhD in counselor education from Virginia Polytechnic Institute and State University, Blacksburg, Virginia; an education specialist degree in school psychology from Radford University, Radford, Virginia; a master of science in psychology from Radford University; and a bachelor of arts in sociology from the University of South Carolina. Dr. Scott has presented many programs on topics of interest to teens such as suicide, adolescent grief and mourning, and stress.